1/27/10

what about...
the natural world?

what about...
the natural world?

Brian Williams

PUBLISHERS

This 2009 edition published and distributed by:
Mason Crest Publishers Inc.
370 Reed Road, Broomall, Pennsylvania 19008
(866) MCP-BOOK (toll free)
www.masoncrest.com

Library of Congress Cataloging-in-Publication data is available

What About...The Natural World
ISBN 978-1-4222-1562-3

What About ... - 10 Title Series
ISBN 978-1-4222-1557-9

Printed in the United States of America

First published in 2004 by Miles Kelly Publishing Ltd
Bardfield Centre, Great Bardfield, Essex, CM7 4SL

Copyright © 2004 Miles Kelly Publishing Ltd

Editorial Director Belinda Gallagher
Art Director Jo Brewer
Senior Editor Jenni Rainford
Assistant Editors Lucy Dowling, Teri Mort
Copy Editor Rosalind Beckman
Design Concept John Christopher
Volume Designers Jo Brewer, Michelle Cannatella
Picture Researcher Liberty Newton
Indexer Helen Snaith
Reprints Controller Bethan Ellish
Production Manager Elizabeth Brunwin
Reprographics Anthony Cambray, Liberty Newton, Ian Paulyn

All images from the Miles Kelly Archives

CONTENTS

The Animal Kingdom

8–9

How are living things unique?
What are the main groups of living things?
What are living things made of?
What is an animal's most important activity?
What is a species?

Prehistoric Animals

10–11

Why did the dinosaurs die out?
Which prehistoric animals could fly?
What were baby dinosaurs like?
Which were the most awesome dinosaurs?
What were the biggest land animals of all time?

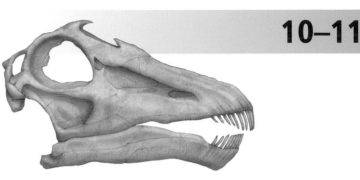

Mammals

12–13

Which mammals lay eggs?
Do pouched animals live only in Australia?
What are carnivores?
Which mammals live in the sea?
How do mammals give birth?
Which is the biggest group of mammals?

Birds

14–15

Which bird has the longest wingspan?
Are all birds able to fly?
Why do birds have beaks?
Do polar bears like to eat penguins?
Why do songbirds sing?

Reptiles and Amphibians

16–17

How many reptiles are there?
How big can reptiles grow?
What are amphibians?
How do snakes hunt?
How long do tortoises live?
Which lizards can change color?

Fish   18–19

How many fish species are there?
Why does a dogfish have no bones?
Which river fish can strip meat from bones in minutes?
What is a coelacanth?
What do deep-sea fish look like?
What is a devilfish?

Invertebrate Animals   20–21

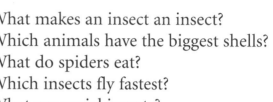

What makes an insect an insect?
Which animals have the biggest shells?
What do spiders eat?
Which insects fly fastest?
What are social insects?

Endangered Animals   22–23

What is the greatest threat to wildlife?
Why is the koala at risk?
Which pigeons went missing for ever?
Why is oil in the water a killer to seabirds?
How can cutting off horns save some animals?

Plants and Fungi   24–25

What are the most abundant plants?
Which plants have no flowers?
How do fungi grow?
How can plants live in water?
What is the tallest grass?

Flowering Plants   26–27

Which are the biggest flowering plants?
How do plants live in dry deserts?
Why does a sprouting plant grow upward?
Why do flowers have bright colors?
Why do some plants have wings and parachutes?
How do plants survive on windy mountains?

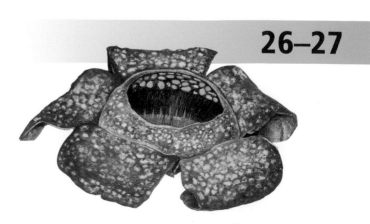

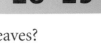

Trees and Shrubs 28–29

Why do some trees lose their leaves?
How can you tell a bush from a shrub?
Why do trees have bark?
Where are the biggest forests?
Why do conifer trees bear cones?

Using Plants 30–31

Why are sunflowers useful as well as pretty?
What are tubers?
Which plants are staple foods?
Which parts of plants can we eat?
How is rice cultivated?
Can we eat seaweed?

Natural Strategies 32–33

Where do marine turtles lay their eggs?
Why do some animals hibernate?
Why do some mammals live in groups?
Why do animals build homes?
What is migration?

Animal and Plant Records 34–35

What is the world's fastest animal?
What is the world's biggest big cat?
What is the largest cactus?
Which are the most deadly sea animals?
What are the smallest animals?

Quiz Time 36–37

Index 38–40

Life on Earth began over 3.5 billion years ago. How? Perhaps by chemical processes within the primeval "soup" of elements; maybe by a haphazard collision of lifeless molecules; possibly by the impact of "seeds" of life-bearing dust from outer space. Life began in the oceans and the oldest known forms of life are fossils of bacteria and algae. Today, there are at least two million species of living organisms on Earth.

How are living things unique?

Only living things can reproduce to make identical copies of themselves. The first living cell, bobbing in the ocean millions of years ago, was unlike anything else on the planet. It used chemical energy in seawater to feed and was able to reproduce.

⬆ *The gorilla is a primate, one of the most advanced of all animals. Yet it is made up of cells, just like the simplest forms of life.*

⬆ *The prehistory of the Earth is divided into very long periods of time called eras, and shorter ones called periods. This is a scene from the Jurassic Period, when plants and animals were very different from those today.*

What are the main groups of living things?

The two main groups of living things are animals and plants. There are five groups, or biological kingdoms. The other three groups are monera, protists (both microscopic one-celled organisms), and fungi. All living things are given names to identify them.

What are living things made of?

All living things are made of cells, which are like tiny chemical factories. Most cells can be seen only through a microscope. Our bodies, and those of every animal and plant, are made of many cells. The simplest plants and animals, such as diatoms, have just one cell, while plants, such as trees, or mammals, such as whales and humans, consist of many millions of cells.

⬇ *Diatoms are very simple life-forms, with just one cell. Most are less than 0.3 in. in size. They float in the oceans, trapping energy from sunlight by a process called photosynthesis.*

⬅ *An amoeba is a single-celled organism that reproduces by dividing to create two new cells. There are many kinds of amoeba. Some live in water; others are parasites, living inside the bodies of animals.*

Evolution **facts**

Gradual change

Evolution is the process of slow change that takes place in animals and plants. Living things seldom stay the same. As habitats change, so do living things in order to survive. Over time, evolutionary changes may produce new species that look different from their ancestors.

⬇ *Many mammal species died out by 10,000 years ago, at the end of the last Ice Age. But many survived, including horses. Modern horses have evolved from prehistoric ancestors that had long legs and more toes.*

DNA

Cells reproduce by dividing. Each new cell gets a copy of the genetic program, the master plan controlling what that cell does. This program is contained in a chemical structure called DNA (deoxyribonucleic acid). It is DNA that determines what species of living thing is created.

What is an animal's most important activity?

For most animals, finding food is the most important activity. Unlike plants, which use energy in sunlight to make their food, animals have to seek out food to provide their bodies with the energy they need. Animals eat different types of food. Herbivores eat only plant food, carnivores eat other animals, and omnivores eat both plants and meat.

⊙ *Male mandrills have colorful red and blue markings on their face as a display to attract females, while females have more muted colored markings. The mandrill spends much of its time looking for food, such as fruits, seeds, eggs, and small animals.*

⊙ *There are only three species of elephants alive today: the African elephant (left), the recently discovered African forest elephant, and the smaller Asian elephant (right). Other species of elephant existed in earlier times.*

What is a species?

A species is one kind of living thing. Male and female of the same species (two African elephants, for example) can breed. Individuals of different species (an African and an Asian elephant) cannot reproduce. Scientists use classification, in terms of species and genus, to group living things by appearance and relationship. So, for example, all red foxes belong to the same species and would be able to reproduce with one another. The red, gray, Arctic, and all other foxes are then placed among the fox genus (with the Latin name *Vulpes*). The fox genus is then part of the larger dog family (*Canidae*).

Oldest **living things**

Species	Years old
Algae and bacteria	3.5 billion
Crustaceans	600 million
Mollusks	500 million
Fish	480 million
Nonflowering plants	400 million
Insects and spiders	370 million
Amphibians	350 million
Reptiles	290 million
Mammals	190 million
Flowering plants	140 million

⊙ *The walrus is from the pinniped group of mammals that includes seals and sea lions. The walrus is a clumsy mover but can support itself in an upright position on land.*

Animal **groups**

Number of species within these animal groups

Insects	1,000,000
Plants	375,000
Arachnids	110,000
Roundworms	100,000
Mollusks	50,000
Fish	27,000
Crustaceans	26,000
Birds	9,000
Reptiles	6,500
Mammals	4,500

For about 160 million years (from 225 million years ago to 65 million years ago) dinosaurs were the most successful animals on Earth. The giant dinosaurs were the biggest reptiles of all time, and were much bigger than elephants. Flying prehistoric reptiles were the biggest animals ever to take to the air. As well as land giants, there were also reptile monsters in the oceans.

⬆ *Like many dinosaurs,* Herrerasaurus *had flaps of skin on its neck, back, and tail. Early fossil studies missed these faint impressions.*

Why did the dinosaurs die out?

The most likely explanation for the extinction of the dinosaurs is that a comet, asteroid, or meteorite hit the Earth. There have been other extinctions in Earth's history, but the disappearance of the dinosaurs around 65 million years ago was a cataclysmic event. Dust clouds flung up by the impact caused climate change: Plants died, eggs failed to hatch, and mature animals died of starvation or cold.

⬇ *A* Maiasaura *mother watches over her eggs as the young hatch.*

Which prehistoric animals could fly?

Insects and some reptiles. There were dragonflies as big as pigeons in prehistoric swamp forests. Flying reptiles, called *Pterosaurs*, flew with bat-like wings of skin stretched between bony fingers. The flying reptile *Quetzalcoatlus* was as big as a small plane with a wingspan of 49 ft. The bird-like reptile *Archaeopteryx* had feathers, but scientists believe that it would not have been able to fly very well.

⬆ Archaeopteryx *lived in the trees, hunting insects. It probably flew no more than a few yards between branches.*

What were baby dinosaurs like?

Like miniversions of their parents. Being reptiles, dinosaurs laid eggs. Some dinosaurs, such as *Maiasaura*, were careful parents. They made nests, guarded their eggs against predators, and stayed with the young until they were able to fend for themselves.

Dinosaur **data**

Dino defenses
Plant-eating dinosaurs were preyed on by the fierce meat eaters, but they had effective defenses in the form of armor plating, shields, spikes, and club tails. Neck frills and horns protected the slow-moving Ceratopsians or "horn-faced" dinosaurs from predator's teeth.

⬅ Triceratops *was the largest of the ceratopsians.*

⬅ Styracosaurus *had frilled horns with bony centers that weighed heavily on the neck.*

⬅ Chasmosaurus *had large bumps called tubercules scattered among its scales.*

Biggest **dinosaurs ever**

Seismosaurus	up to 160 ft. long, 55–90 tons
Antarctosaurus	100 ft., 55–90 tons
Brachiosaurus	80 ft., 55 tons
Diplodocus	75 ft., 13 tons
Apatosaurus	65 ft., 22–33 tons

Which were the most awesome dinosaurs?

The most frightening of all the dinosaurs that lived were the giant meat-eaters. *Tyrannosaurus rex* was up to 42 ft. long, 20 ft. in height and 6.5 tons in weight. *Tyrannosaurus'* mouth opened so wide it could have swallowed a 10-year-old child with ease. A second giant, *Allosaurus*, was up to 40 ft. long, weighed up to 6.5 tons, and had enormous jaws that were lined with incredibly sharp teeth. But just as awesome and savagely fierce were the smaller killers, which included the vicious "slashing claw" *Deinonychus* and the smaller *Stenonychosaurus*. The human-sized *Velociraptor* was even capable of working as a team to bring down a much bigger dinosaur. These crafty carnivores were likely to have been some of the most intelligent dinosaurs around.

⬇ Brachiosaurus *had a very long tail and a long neck, which it probably used to reach treetop foliage to feed on. This dinosaur giant could grow up to 80 ft. long.*

⬆ Tyrannosaurus *preyed on weaker dinosaurs, and also ate carrion (dead animals).*

What were the biggest land animals of all time?

Prehistoric reptilian sauropods, such as *Seismosaurus* and *Brachiosaurus*. These 55-ton reptiles were as big as houses. They lived in herds, ate plants, and had very long necks to reach up to nibble on treetops. Evidence from fossil footprints also suggests that they were able to run quite fast. *Mamenchisaurus*, a herbivore (plant-eater) whose bones have been found in China, had a neck 50 ft. long. Some of these giants had tails even longer than their necks. The biggest land mammal was *Baluchitherium*, a kind of mega-rhinoceros weighing 33 tons. The largest land animal of today, the modern African elephant, weighs only 7.5 tons!

Shake those hips

Scientists divide dinosaurs into two groups, according to their skeletons. Saurischians had "reptile-hipped" bones, while Ornithischians had hip bones shaped more like those of birds. It is probable that modern birds are descended from dinosaurs. Their scaly feet are similar to those of the dinosaurs.

Ornithischian hip bones

Saurischian hip bones

Amazing **facts**

- *Ankylosaurus* was 33 ft. long, and had a club-like tail.

- *Stegosaurus* was about 23 ft. long, with a spiky tail and plates on its back.

- *Triceratops* was about 30 ft. long, with a bony neck frill and three horns: It had the biggest skull of any animal.

- *Spinosaurus* measured up to 39 ft. long and weighed as much as 5.5 tons.

Mammals are not the biggest group of animals. But they are amazingly adaptable, and live in a wide range of habitats—on land, in the ocean and in the air—and in all sorts of climates. They have bigger brains (in relation to their body size) than other animals. The biggest sea and land animals are mammals—whales in the ocean and elephants on dry land.

⬆ *The platypus lives in rivers in western Australia. It has webbed feet and a paddle tail for swimming.*

Which mammals lay eggs?

The only egg-laying mammals are the duckbilled platypus and the five species of spiny anteaters, or echidnas. These curious animals live only in Australia. The female platypus lays two eggs in a burrow, and suckles the young when they hatch. The female echidna lays one egg into a pouch on her body and the baby grows inside, sucking milk from her fur.

Do pouched animals live only in Australia?

No, some live in New Guinea and the Solomon Islands of the Pacific Ocean, and two kinds (opossums and rat opossums) live in the Americas. Mammals with pouches for rearing their young are called marsupials. Australia has the largest variety of marsupial animals, which includes kangaroos, koalas, wallabies, possums, wombats, and bandicoots.

⬅ *A baby kangaroo (a joey) grows inside its mother's pouch. It climbs back inside for safety until it grows too big for the pouch.*

What are carnivores?

Carnivores are flesh-eating hunting animals. Some of the best known hunters are the big cats—lions, tigers, leopards, jaguars, cheetahs—and many smaller cats. Most cats hunt alone, using stealth. Other families of carnivores include the dogs (wolves, jackals, and foxes) and the weasels (otters, badgers, mink). Many marine animals such as sharks and dolphins, are carnivores, hunting and feeding on fish and other living things in the water.

➡ *A leopard usually hunts at night, and after a kill drags its meal into a tree out of reach of scavengers such as hyenas.*

Marvellous **mammals**

Mammal giants
There are about 4,500 mammal species, ranging in size from whales to tiny shrews and bats. Biggest of all is the gigantic blue whale, which can grow to 110 ft. long and weigh more than 140 tons.

Biggest **hoofed animals**

Name	Height	Weight
White rhinoceros	6 ft.	6,600 lb.
Hippopotamus	5 ft.	3,000 lb.
Giraffe	18 ft.	2,600 lb.

Intelligent **mammals**

The most intelligent animals (not including humans):
1. Chimpanzee
2. Gorilla
3. Orangutan
4. Baboon
5. Dolphin

⬆ *Scientists assess a dolphin's reaction to various sights, sounds, and situations in order to gauge their intelligence.*

Which mammals live in the sea?

Seals, dolphins, and whales are sea mammals whose ancestors lived on land millions of years ago. Their front legs have become flippers or paddles for swimming, and instead of back legs whales have horizontal tail fins, or flukes. Seals and sea lions can still move on land, but whales and dolphins are now entirely water animals.

Like dolphins and other whales, killer whales are intelligent animals.

How do mammals give birth?

The placental mammals (the biggest mammal group) give birth to live young. Inside the female's body the developing young are nourished by an organ called the placenta. Most mammal babies are fairly well developed when born, though they still need parental care to begin with.

This baby rhino is a miniature replica of its massive mother, but will need her protection during the early months of its life.

Which is the biggest group of mammals?

Surprisingly, bats. There are 960 species of bats—the only mammals that truly fly. The largest bats are the fruit bats and flying foxes, which can have wings almost 7 ft. across, but most bats are small, about the size of a mouse. Many bats are nocturnal insect-eaters, but some also prey on small rodents, frogs, and fish. Night-flying bats use echolocation to find their way in the dark and to locate prey. They send out high-pitched squeaks that are reflected as echoes from nearby objects.

Many bats have extra-large ears to pick up echoes as "sonic images." The bat homes in on its target, such as a moth. Many bats roost together in colonies, sleeping upside down, dangling from their foot claws.

Longest **gestation periods**

It takes a long time for a mammal baby to develop: nine months for a human, but even longer for other large mammals.

Elephant	660 days
Whale	500 days
Walrus	480 days
Rhinoceros	450 days
Giraffe	430 days

Mammal **champions**

Record	Held by
Biggest rodent	Capybara (as big as a goat)
Biggest ungulate (one-toed or hooved mammal)	Hippopotamus
Longest hair	Yak (hair up to 3 ft.)
Largest bear	Polar bear (1,100 lb.)
Smelliest mammal	Skunk
Sleepiest mammal	Dormouse
Slowest-moving mammal	Sloth
Heaviest tree-dwelling mammal	Orangutan (up to 200 lb.)
Mammal most at home in mountains	Pika (up to 20,000 ft. altitude)
Most armored mammal	Armadillos and pangolins

Birds are warm-blooded vertebrates (animals with backbones). Their feathers keep them warm and help them to fly. They walk on two back legs, while their front limbs have become wings. All birds lay eggs. And all birds' bodies are strong but light, ideal for flying—though not all birds fly.

↑ The graceful albatross glides through the air over the vast southern oceans, seldom having to beat its wings.

Which bird has the longest wingspan?

The wandering albatross of the southern oceans has the longest wingspan with long, thin wings that can measure more than 10 ft. from wingtip to wingtip. Its wings enable it to glide for enormous distances with little muscular effort. These majestic birds cannot take off very easily, so they launch themselves into "upcurrents" of air from their clifftop nests. The marabou stork comes a close second with a wingspan of almost 10 ft.

Are all birds able to fly?

No, some birds have wings that are useless for flying. Some run or creep about, while others have wings adapted for swimming. Flightless land birds live in Africa (ostrich), South America (rhea), and Australia and New Guinea (emu and cassowary). The small, flightless kiwi lives in the forests of New Zealand, which was once home to a much bigger, flightless bird, the giant moa.

↓ The ostrich relies on fast running to escape enemies, but it can also give a vicious kick.

Birds of a feather

Feathered friends
Feathers are made of a horn-like protein called keratin, the same stuff your hair and nails are made of, but feathers are very light and very strong. A swan has about 25,000 feathers. Hummingbirds, which look as if they have scales not feathers, have the fewest of any bird—less than 1,000.

→ A bird's skeleton is very light to help it glide through the air easily.

Design secrets
Bird bones are hollow but reinforced with cross struts to withstand the twists and turns of flight. Birds have very efficient lungs and their digestive system works very fast because flying takes a lot of energy.

↓ In flight, a bird's flapping wings make circular and up-and-down movements—the wing tips pushing forward on the upstroke.

↑ *A chinstrap penguin chases fish, using its wings like oars to "row" through the water.*

↓ *Storks, such as this yellow-billed stork, use their long beaks to probe for food in shallow waters and marshes.*

Why do birds have beaks?

The bird jaw has become a beak, which has adapted to catch and eat all kinds of food. Reptiles and mammals have teeth, but birds do not. Birds of prey have hooked beaks, for tearing flesh. Fish-eaters such as herons have long spear beaks. There are specialized beaks designed for seed-eaters, nut-crackers, fruit-pickers, and insect-snappers. Some birds also use their beaks as tools to make nests or to bore holes.

➔ *The song thrush has one of the most melodious songs of all European birds.*

Do polar bears like to eat penguins?

They never get the chance. Polar bears are the top land predator of the northern hemisphere polar lands (the Arctic), while penguins live in the southern seas, as far south as Antarctica. Penguins cannot fly but their wings have evolved into flippers for swimming. A penguin is streamlined to dart after fish—and escape hungry leopard seals and killer whales.

Why do songbirds sing?

Birds sing to tell other birds where they are, or to defend their territory— where they nest and find food. Singing is the bird's way of telling other birds to "keep out." Singing also helps male birds to attract females during the breeding season. Early morning in spring is a good time to hear birdsong, but some birds sing at dusk, too.

Oldest birds

In the wild, small birds have many predators. Many are killed in their first year. Bigger birds tend to live longer. Birds kept in captivity and wild birds ringed by scientists are studied to discover how long they can live. A Siberian white crane, a sulphur-crested cockatoo, and a goose have been recorded to reach 80 years old.

Take off

Taking off for most birds involves flapping the wings to produce thrust and lift. Broad, rounded wings give the best lift and acceleration— useful for escaping a predator. Big birds, such as geese, run into the wind to generate enough lift to take off. Birds with long, narrow wings, such as swallows, can only take off from a high point— falling into the air and letting the air carry them.

Birdbrained or bright?

Ravens and pigeons can work out simple counting sums. Parrots, budgerigars, and mynahs can mimic human speech (though that is not the same as talking), and some parrots can name and count objects. The Galapagos woodpecker finch uses a twig as a tool to extract grubs from tree bark.

Birds' eggs

The ostrich lays the biggest egg. An ostrich egg is 8 in. long, and would be big enough to make 24 omelettes. The smallest bird egg, at 0.4 in. long, is laid by the hummingbird.

Reptiles and amphibians are cold-blooded animals, which means they need sunshine to warm their bodies, and so are not found in really cold climates. In cool climates, these animals often hibernate during the winter. Many amphibians are water creatures, but reptiles are found in dry deserts, rainforests, swamps, and even in saltwater oceans.

Crocodiles, such as this Indian gharial, hunt in the water, grabbing land animals and also preying on fish and water creatures.

How many reptiles are there?

More than 6,500 species. There are more lizards than any other reptiles—about 3,700 species. Next come the snakes (2,800). The biggest living reptile belongs to one of the smaller reptile families—the crocodiles—with only 25 species. There are about 3,000 species of amphibians, most of them frogs and toads. In general, amphibians are smaller than reptiles.

This picture shows some reptiles and amphibians. The poison arrow frog is small but deadly. The Komodo dragon (the biggest lizard) and Nile crocodile are giants by comparison and highly dangerous carnivores.

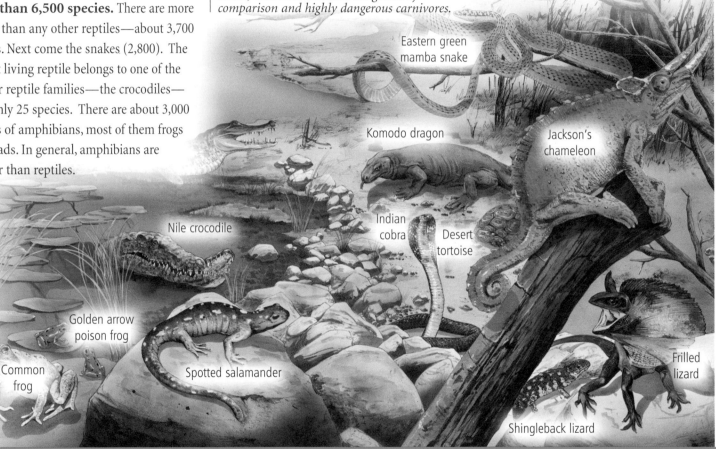

Eastern green mamba snake

Komodo dragon

Jackson's chameleon

Nile crocodile

Indian cobra

Desert tortoise

Golden arrow poison frog

Spotted salamander

Common frog

Frilled lizard

Shingleback lizard

Head to tail **facts**

Throwaway tails

Lizards have many enemies. Some run away, other lizards stay still and hide. Others try to make themselves look bigger and fiercer. Some lizards shed their tails when in danger so that the predator is distracted by the wriggling tail while the tailless lizard escapes.

The frilled lizard raises a neck frill of skin to make itself look bigger to predators.

Eggs

Amphibian eggs have to be laid in water, otherwise they would dry out. Reptiles are better adapted to land life, because reptile eggs have tough skins to protect the developing young. Crocodiles watch over their nest, taking good care of the baby crocs.

Alligator egg

Python egg

Biggest crocs

The world's longest crocodile is the estuarine crocodile (23 ft. long), which lives in Southeast Asia and Australia, and sometimes swims far out to sea. The Indian gharial is 20 ft. long, the Nile crocodile and the American crocodile are 16 ft. long, and the American alligator is 13 ft.

How big can reptiles grow?

A large crocodile can weigh as much as 1,000 lb. and live more than a hundred years. As a reptile heavyweight, only a leatherback turtle outweighs a crocodile. The biggest lizard is the Komodo dragon, up to 10 ft. long. The longest reptiles are snakes. In 1912 a dead python was measured at 33 ft. long. The heaviest snake is the anaconda, at 440 lb.

⬆ *Snakes, such as this pit viper, have heat sensing pits in its head, to track prey in the dark or underground.*

What are amphibians?

Amphibians include frogs, toads, newts and salamanders. They can live on land or in water, and most return to water to lay their eggs, even if they spend most of their life on dry land. The eggs hatch into tadpoles, which grow legs and become adult animals, able to live on land or water. Amphibians were the first animals to move onto dry land in prehistoric times.

➡ *Frogs mate in the water and lay clusters of eggs in a jellylike mass of spawn.*

How do snakes hunt?

Snakes have poor eyesight and hunt mainly by using smell, sounds, and special heat detecting organs on their heads. Some snakes, like grass snakes, simply grab prey with their sharp teeth. Others, such as boas and pythons, kill by constriction (crushing the prey until it cannot breathe). Many snakes kill by biting with curved fangs, which inject deadly poison. All snakes swallow their food whole.

How long do tortoises live?

As long as a hundred years. A tortoise given to the ruler of Tonga by Captain Cook some time before 1777 lived until 1965, so it was at least 188 years old. Tortoises move slowly—they have no need to dash around because they carry protective shells with them. This slow lifestyle means tortoises use only a small amount of energy, and so can live on very poor vegetation.

Which lizards can change color?

Chameleons are tree lizards and can change color (camouflage) to match their surroundings for protection. They also change color when alarmed or angry. Chameleons catch insects by uncoiling very long, sticky tongues at high speed. They also have eyes that swivel independently to give them the best all-round vision of any reptile.

➡ *Chameleons move slowly, clinging onto branches with their claws.*

⬇ *Axolotls live in lakes and can spend their entire lives in water. If the lake dries up, however, the axolotls "grow up" to become salamanders, able to move about on land.*

Amazing **reptile facts**

- Gecko lizards can crawl across ceilings because they have hairy feet and each hair tip contains thousands of microscopic "stickers."

- The tadpole of a South American frog is three times bigger than the adult. In contrast to most living things, as it grows older, it gets smaller!

- The southern African rain frog lives underground and only comes to the surface when it rains. It cannot swim.

- You can usually tell whether a reptile is active by day or by night from its eyes. If the pupil (the black part in the center of the eye) is a slit that closes almost completely in sunlight, the animal is nocturnal (active by night). A wide, round pupil means a reptile is active by day.

Fish are the animals most perfectly adapted to living in water. They swim better than any other animal, and they can breathe by means of gills rather than lungs. Fish can live in salty water (the ocean) or fresh water (rivers, lakes, and pools). Some fish, such as eels and salmon, live in both. Sea fish tend to grow bigger than river and lake fish.

How many fish species are there?

Fish are the most numerous vertebrate animals (animals with backbones) and there are thought to be over 22,000 species. About a third of these species live in fresh water. There are three main groups of fish: jawless fish (such as hagfish); cartilaginous fish (sharks and rays); and bony fish—the biggest group.

⬇A shoal of yellow snapper. Swimming in shoals means a small fish stands a better chance of avoiding becoming a predator's next meal.

⬆The dogfish is a small relative of the great white shark.

Why does a dogfish have no bones?

A dogfish is a small shark and all sharks have a skeleton made of gristly material called cartilage. It is similar to bone, but more bendy and not so hard. Sharks have very rough skins, too, like sandpaper to the touch and, unlike bony fishes, they have no swim bladder to enable them to float without swimming.

Which river fish can strip meat from bones in minutes?

Many stories (mostly untrue) are told of fierce sharks, but the small piranha has razor sharp teeth for chopping out flesh in chunks. This small fish lives in the rivers of South America. Unlike most predatory fish, piranhas hunt in shoals (groups). A shoal of piranhas can strip the flesh off a pig in less than a minute, leaving just the carcass.

➡The piranha is small, but ferocious when hungry.

⬇The coelacanth has been around since the time of the dinosaurs.

What is a coelacanth?

The coelacanth is a marine "living fossil." Scientists thought this primitive-looking fish died out 70 million years ago—until in 1938 a coelacanth was caught off East Africa. Since then, coelacanths have also been found living on the eastern side of the Indian Ocean, off the islands of Indonesia.

Fishy facts

➡The ocean sunfish is the heaviest bony fish. It lays an astonishing number of eggs—about 300 million. Most get eaten by other fish and sea animals.

Sharks

The biggest fish is the whale shark. It can grow up to 60 ft. from the tip of its tail to its big, gaping mouth. But this 16-ton monster is a gentle giant and eats only tiny plankton. Some of its relatives are among the most powerful predators in the natural world. They include the mako shark, which grows up to 11 ft.; the white shark (16 ft.); the tiger shark, and the hammerhead (16 ft.). All of these sharks have been known to attack people in the water.

Whale shark

What do deep-sea fish look like?

Some look very strange. Their world is black and cold—no sunlight filters down below around 2,500 ft. Food is scarce, so many deep-sea fish have wide gaping mouths to make sure of catching whatever prey comes near. Some use "fishing rods" to attract prey. Many deep-sea fish have special organs to make their own "bio-light," to help identify one another in the darkness.

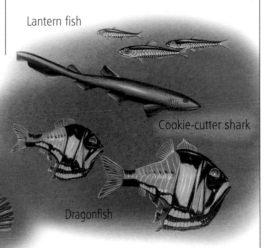

Many deep-sea fish glow to confuse predators.

Lantern fish

Cookie-cutter shark

Dragonfish

Anglerfish are dark colored for camouflage, but a glowing tip extends from its dorsal fin to attract prey.

The viperfish has a lure and huge jaws to grab the next meal, while lanternfish make their own light.

What is a devilfish?

This is another name for the giant manta ray. The manta ray looks fearsome, with a "wing" span of up to 23 ft. across. Sailors in the past told stories of mantas rising up out of the ocean to shroud a ship in their wings and drag it underwater. In fact, the manta is a harmless giant that will even allow divers to hitch a lift clinging on to its body. The manta has broad fins for swimming effortlessly through the water, using its "horns" to guide plankton into its gaping mouth.

The manta is the largest of the rays. Rays and skates are fish with flattened bodies, and are related to sharks.

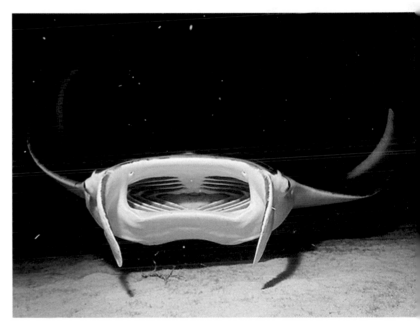

Fishy tails and scales

Fish swim using a side-to-side movement of their bodies. Muscles make up approximately 70 percent of a fish's weight. A fish uses its fins for steering—the tail fin, for example, acts as a rudder. Like all animals, fish need oxygen—but they take in oxygen, which is dissolved in water, through their gills. The older a fish is, the bigger its scales—as the fish gets bigger, its scales get bigger, too.

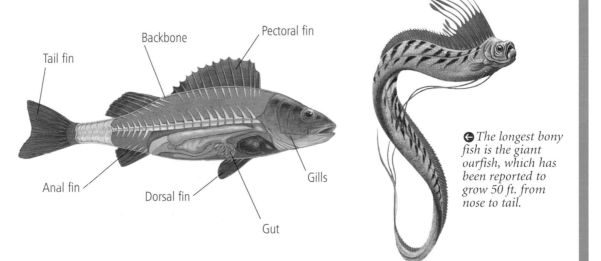

Tail fin

Backbone

Pectoral fin

Anal fin

Dorsal fin

Gills

Gut

The longest bony fish is the giant oarfish, which has been reported to grow 50 ft. from nose to tail.

There are two main groups of animals—animals with backbones (vertebrates) and animals without backbones (invertebrates). About 96 percent of all animals are invertebrates—they include insects, spiders, crustaceans, mollusks, worms, starfish, and corals. Insects can live almost anywhere and eat almost anything. It is just as well that their body design limits their size, so that giant insects exist only in horror films.

The bolas spider twirls its thread around to catch a moth, and then hauls in its meal.

What makes an insect an insect?

Every insect has three pairs of legs and a body that is divided into three parts: head, thorax (middle), and abdomen. All insects have certain features in common. On the head are eyes, mouth parts, and a pair of antennae or feelers. Most, though not all, insects have wings.

A bombardier beetle, like all insects, has six legs. This beetle has an unusual defensive weapon— it sprays a jet of hot gas at an enemy.

Which animals have the biggest shells?

Giant clams in warm oceans have the biggest shells—over 3 ft. across. Insects have hard bodies, but many mollusks, such as snails and cone shells, have elaborate, decorative shells. Crustaceans (crabs, lobsters, and shrimps) also have shells. Like insects, crustaceans are arthropods (animals with jointed legs), and most of them live in the sea.

The hermit crab has a soft body, and so makes its home inside the empty shell of a mollusk.

What do spiders eat?

All spiders are carnivores, and most feed on insects and other small creatures. Spiders catch their food in a variety of ways; some just chase their prey, but many spiders make silk web traps to snare their victims. The bolas spider dangles a sticky ball from a silk thread. The sticky ball gives off a chemical smell similar to a female moth to attract male moths flying nearby. When the moth flies in, it gets stuck to the ball.

Intriguing **insects**

Metamorphosis
Many insects, such as butterflies and moths, experience a complete metamorphosis when developing into an adult insect. All insects lay eggs. Butterflies and moths lay their eggs on plants, on which their young—the larvae or caterpillar—start to feed as soon as they hatch. The next stage in the process is when the caterpillar spins a cocoon around itself to become a chrysalis. Inside, a transformation takes place and from the chrysalis an adult insect emerges in the form of a butterfly or moth.

Insect **numbers**

Insect	No. of species
Beetles	400,000
Butterflies and moths	165,000
Ants, bees, wasps	140,000
Flies	120,000
Bugs	90,000

The caterpillar makes a cocoon and becomes a chrysalis. An adult butterfly emerges to start the cycle all over again.

Dragonfly can fly
swiftly with a set
of four wings

Thorax

Abdomen

Head

↑ *Dragonflies catch other insects in midair, using their front legs as a "net." They have eyes larger than any other insect to be able to spot prey.*

Which insects fly fastest?

The fastest fliers in the insect world are dragonflies, which can speed along at up to 60 mph when in pursuit of their next meal. Second fastest are the botflies, flying at around 30 mph. The bumblebee flies at speeds of about 11 mph.

What are social insects?

A few species of insects live in groups, or colonies, making them social insects. These insects include honeybees, some wasps, and all ants and termites. All the members work for the good of the colony, helping to build a nest and care for the young. Ants work together with the use of chemical pheromones that send signals among the group. One beehive in summer will contain one queen, up to 60,000 worker bees, and a few hundred fertile males. Only one individual female, the queen, lays eggs.

← *It takes 21 days for a bee to develop from an egg to an adult.*

↑ *Honeybees build nests of wax sheets called combs. Brood cells in the comb contain grubs that hatch from the eggs laid by the queen.*

Insect **record breakers**

Biggest insect	Birdwing butterfly and Atlas moth—1 ft. across
Heaviest insect	Goliath beetle—3.5 ounces
Longest insect	Stick insect—16 in. long
Fastest runner	Tropical cockroach—more than 3 mph

Chomping jaws

Praying mantids are fussy eaters. Usually, they will only eat other insects that they have captured alive. They hold their spiny front legs together as if praying—then grab the victim and start to chew.

Amazing **insect facts**

• There are at least one million known insect species, and some scientists think there could be up to ten million species.

• Insects, such as ants, can drag objects many times heavier than themselves. They can construct enormous homes, such as the termites' mound.

• A flea can jump 130 times its own height, and a caterpillar has six times more muscles than a human.

• A rhinoceros beetle can carry up to 850 times its own weight!

← *A green mantis from Malaysia settles down to a meal.*

Thousands of animals have died out naturally in the course of evolution. Several mass extinctions happened in prehistoric times—the biggest was 240 million years ago, when perhaps 96 percent of living things vanished. Another, 65 million years ago, saw the disappearance of the dinosaurs. The rate of extinction has accelerated in the last 200 years and today over 5,000 species are endangered.

Why is the koala at risk?

Because it is a specialized feeder. This Australian marsupial eats only eucalyptus tree leaves. Being dependent on one food source is dangerous, because if the forests are cut down, the koalas cannot find anywhere else to live, or anything else to eat. A similar threat faces the Chinese giant panda, whose diet is mainly bamboo shoots. A shortage of bamboo means starvation for pandas.

What is the greatest threat to wildlife?

Habitat loss is the most serious threat to endangered animals and plants. For example, when tropical rainforests are felled for timber or agriculture, most of the wildlife dependent on the rainforest cannot survive anywhere else. They cannot find food or breed, and so their numbers start to decline. Many lost species are insects and other

⬆ *A snow leopard needs a large hunting territory. Human interference, hunting for the fur trade and loss of its natural prey make survival difficult for big predators.*

invertebrates never studied by scientists. Changes to farm methods, housebuilding, hotel developments along the beaches, and overhunting all threaten wild species.

➥ *Koalas survived hunting in the early 20th century and are now a protected species.*

Endangered and **extinct**

Key **dates**

1870 North American bison almost wiped out by hunting.
1872 Yellowstone National Park (USA).
1935 White whales protected from hunting by whalers.
1961 World Wildlife Fund (now Worldwide Fund for Nature) founded.
1975 First international convention on banning trade in products from endangered animals.

1989 *Exxon Valdez* oil spill in Alaska—not the first oil spill, but it raised public awareness.
1997 More than 5,000 species listed as endangered by the International Union for the Conservation of Nature and Natural Resources.

➥ *Marine turtles face threat from fishing nets at sea and tourists on their breeding beaches.*

⬆ *The giant panda lives in China and feeds on a specialized diet of bamboo. Its numbers have never been large, and attempts to breed giant pandas in captivity have not been very successful.*

Which pigeons went missing for ever?

A flightless pigeon called the dodo lived undisturbed on the island of Mauritius in the Indian Ocean until European sailors arrived in the 1500s. Sailors killed the birds for food, rats and cats ate the eggs, and by 1680 the dodo was extinct. The most unexpected extinction was that of the passenger pigeon. Billions of these birds lived in North America until hunters began killing pigeons for food. Between 1850 and 1880 the vast flocks vanished and the last passenger pigeon died in a zoo in 1914.

⊕ The dodo was flightless and had no defense against humans or introduced predators.

⊕ Rhino horn is wrongly believed by some to possess magical properties, so the horns are used in medicine and in making weapons.

Why is oil in the water a killer to seabirds?

Seabirds that come into contact with the greasy surface of oily water cannot fly because their feathers become clogged with oil. This means that the birds cannot hunt to feed and soon die. Some birds are rescued by conservationists and cleaned up in order to be able to fly again, and eventually returned to the wild.

How can cutting off horns save some animals?

Removing the horns from rhinos living in game reserves does not hurt the animals, nor affect their lives seriously, but it makes them less of a target for poachers. Poachers in Africa kill rhinos for their horns, which are actually made of hair. The horns are used in traditional medicines in some countries, and in the making of ornamental weapons, such as knives. Poaching for rhino horn, elephant tusks, and even elephants' feet is a serious problem in parts of Africa. By removing a rhino's horn, poachers have no need to hunt and kill them.

⊕ This seabird died as a result of having wings clogged with oil, which made it unable to fly and hunt for food.

Extinct **species**

- The great auk was called the "penguin of the north." It was hunted for its eggs and skins, and the last one was killed in 1844.

- Diatryma was a carnivorous flightless bird, 6 ft. tall and fierce enough to eat a pony!

- Megatherium was a ground sloth as big as an elephant.

- Glyptodon was an armadillo as big as a rhinoceros.

- Diprotodon was a giant Australian wombat, as big as a bear.

- Steller's sea cow was related to the manatee. It was 23 ft. long and weighed 11 tons. It was killed off in the 1700s by hunters.

Endangered **species**

African wild dogs—less than 5,500 left.
Californian condor—Numbers fell dramatically until the last pair in the wild were captured for breeding. Numbers have since risen again.
Lions—population in Africa fell from 230,000 in 1980 to under 23,000 in 2003.
Tigers in Asia—less than 10,000 left.
Turtles—declining worldwide.
Wolves and bears—very rare in Europe.

⊕ The giant moa was a huge, flightless bird from New Zealand that was wiped out by people who hunted it for its meat.

There are about 375,000 kinds of plants. The biggest plant family is the flowering plants, or angiosperms, with over 250,000 species. Plants make their own food, using sunlight (photosynthesis). Fungi used to be classed as plants, but since they cannot make their own food, they are now put in a class of their own that includes about 100,000 species.

⊙ *Tropical cycads are primitive cone-bearing plants that look rather like palm trees.*

What are the most abundant plants?

The flowering plants—grasses, cacti, trees, peas and beans, vines, potatoes, and many wild and garden flowers. Flowers help plants to reproduce. The flower produces male and female cells (pollen and egg cells), and it also makes sure that seeds are spread—by attracting animals such as bees. The biggest groups of flowering plants are orchids, 17,000 species; legumes (peas and beans) 16,000 species; and compositae (daisy-like flowers) 14,000 species.

Which plants have no flowers?

Mosses and ferns have no flowers. Instead of seeds, they produce spores, which fall to the ground and develop into a structure called a prothallus—it is this structure that produces male and female cells to make a new plant. Conifers have no flowers either. They are "gymnosperms," and have cones containing pollen and seeds. Male and female cones may be on the same plant, as in most conifers, or on separate plants, as in cycads.

⊙ *Flowering plants, nonflowering plants, and fungi grow together in woodlands.*

Bracket fungus

Birch sapling

Fern

Mushroom

Fly agaric

Bluebell

Cuckoo-pint

Foxglove

Acorn

Surprising plant **facts**

Super seeds
Frozen seeds of the Arctic lupin thawed and started growing in 1966 after scientists reckoned they had been in deep-freeze conditions for 10,000 years.

➲ *A fern reproduces by spores, not by seeds. Ferns are among the oldest plants living on land.*

Photosynthesis
Photosynthesis is the process plants use to make food. The food-producing parts of a green plant contain chlorophyll. Using water and carbon dioxide gas as raw materials, and energy from sunlight (harnessed by the chlorophyll), the plants build up food sugar in their cells.

➲ *Chlorophyll in a plant's leaves makes photosynthesis work. Oxygen and water are given off as the plant makes its food.*

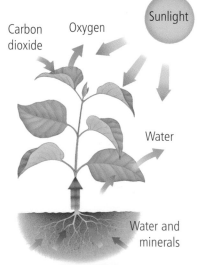

Sunlight

Carbon dioxide

Oxygen

Water

Water and minerals

How do fungi grow?

Fungi take food from other plants or feed as scavengers from dead, decaying matter, such as a fallen tree. Fungi contain no chlorophyll so they cannot make their own food, like green plants. Instead, they can grow on anything made of cellulose—such as food, clothes, wooden furniture, even old books—especially in damp places.

⬇ *Fungi, such as this cattail fungus, produce chemicals that feed on cellulose—the material of which green plant cells are made.*

⬆ *All we see of the water lily is its flower on the surface of the water, but underneath the surface, long stalks connect it to the roots on the river bed, like an anchor.*

How can plants live in water?

Over 90 percent of a plant is water, so it is not surprising that plants manage to live in water perfectly well, so long as they can obtain sunlight. Some plants float on the surface, others root in the bottom of ponds or streams. Seaweeds growing in the oceans are very tough to survive being pounded by waves or being dried and then soaked again as the tides come in and go out on the seashore.

➔ *Instead of a root, a seaweed has a "holdfast" foot that sticks to a rock to keep the plant in one place.*

⬇ *It is hard to imagine a lawn of bamboo, but lawn grass and bamboo are related plants.*

What is the tallest grass?

Bamboo looks like a tree but is actually a giant grass. It is the tallest grass (growing up to 80 ft.) and the fastest-growing plant, shooting up almost 3 ft. a day. Grasses have very small flowers, with no petals, and form the largest group of wind pollinated plants. There are about 10,000 species.

Biggest and oldest **plants**

Biggest leaf	Raffia palm—65 ft.
Biggest seed	Coco de mer palm—44 lb.
Longest seaweed	Giant kelp—65 yd.
Oldest plant	Creosote plant and Antarctic lichen—12,000 years

Amazing **facts**

- A single orchid can make more than 4.5 million seeds.

- A single fungus can produce up to 5 million spores.

- The most deadly fungus is the death cap, *Amanita phalloides*.

Plant **families**

Angiosperms—have enclosed seeds and easily seen flowers.
Gymnosperms—wind-pollinated, "naked seeds" in cones.
Pteridophytes—simple plants, such as ferns, horsetails, and clubmosses.
Bryophytes—liverworts and mosses, the simplest true land plants.
Algae—most live in water; they range from single-celled diatoms to giant seaweeds.

➔ *A few plants are carnivorous. Pitcher plants supplement their diet by catching insects, which fall into the plant's trap.*

Flowering plants are successful because they are good at spreading their seeds and are very adaptable. Flowering plants live in most of the Earth's environments, including hot deserts and high mountains. There are more than 250,000 species of flowering plants, including flowers, vegetables, grasses, trees, and herbs, which are all divided into two main groups: monocotyledons, such as grasses and bulb plants, and the bigger group—dicotyledons.

How do plants live in dry deserts?

Some desert plants have long roots to reach deep underground where the water supply can be found. Others store water in their thick stems and fleshy leaves. Desert plants may look dead until the rain comes when they burst into life, grow and flower—and the desert briefly blooms.

Cactus plants can grow in deserts, providing it rains occasionally.

The huge flower of the rafflesia, which is also called the stinking corpse flower because of its pungent smell used to attract insects.

Which are the biggest flowering plants?

The biggest flower belongs to the smelly rafflesia of Southeast Asia. Its yard-wide flower smells like rotting meat to attract insects. Some flowering plants are enormous—a Chinese wisteria in California has branches 500 ft. long and produces 1.5 million flowers every year.

How plants **work**

Parts of a flower

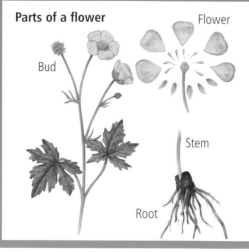

Flower
Bud
Stem
Root

Plants need light

A bulb can be kept in a dark cupboard while it is dormant or beginning to shoot, but if you keep the sprouting plant away from sunlight, it will die. Mushrooms on the other hand, which are fungi, can live in darkness because they get their nourishment from plants or dead matter.

Germination is when a seed starts to grow. It puts out a shoot first. Then the seed leaves emerge, followed by the main stem and proper leaves.

Thirsty plants

Without water, plants wilt and die. Plant cells cannot do their jobs without water, nor can photosynthesis take place to feed the plant. Water also helps keep plant cells rigid. Without enough water, the cells go limp and the plant wilts.

Why does a sprouting plant grow upward?

Because its leaves must reach the sunlight. A plant starts life as a a bulb or seed in the soil. Even if planted upside down, the roots will start to push downward under the influence of gravity. The shoot, bearing the leaves, pushes upward toward the sunlight to start making food for the growing plant.

A tulip starts life as a bulb, which sends out roots and a shoot. The leaves emerge into the sunlight and then, finally, the flower.

Why do flowers have bright colors?

To attract animals, which transfer pollen from one plant to another. This is called cross-pollination. The chief pollinators are insects, which are attracted to flowers by their colors and scents. Insects do not see the same colors as us. To a bee a red flower looks gray, while a white flower probably looks blue. Birds, bats, rodents, and even marsupials pollinate flowers in some parts of the world.

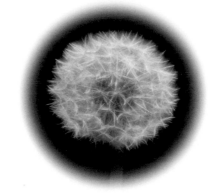

The dandelion produces the familiar fluffy seed head. Blow it to "tell the time," and you are helping the plant spread its seeds.

Why do some plants have wings and parachutes?

To insure the wind can carry a plant's seeds as far from the parent tree as possible. Dandelion seeds are so light that they blow about easily. The fruits of some other plants, such as maple trees, have winged seeds, which spin as they fall from the tree like the rotor blades of a helicopter.

When bees and other insects feed on flowers, pollen sticks to them, which they carry to other flowers of the same species.

How do plants survive on windy mountains?

Plants such as mosses, shrubs, and some flowers can survive the high winds and winter cold of mountains by staying small—they cling close to the ground. They have long roots to hold tight to the soil and to reach down to find as much moisture and food as possible. The trees best suited to alpine heights are conifers.

An alpine meadow in spring with many flowers in bloom.

Transpiration
Plants lose water through tiny pores (holes) called stomata in the undersides of leaves. This is called transpiration and helps keep the plant cool.

Upper leaf layer

Spongy cells

Stomata (leaf pores)

Roots
Roots draw up water from the soil. The flow of water up the plant stem brings with it minerals to feed the plant.

Waterproof wax coat

Leaf veins with tiny tubes

Lower layer of leaf

Inside a leaf: Carbon dioxide gas from the air passes through tiny holes called stomata into the leaf. The leaf gives off oxygen and water.

Plant **defenses**

- Hairy, stinging leaves (like a stinging nettle's) stop hungry animals nibbling them.

- Silica toughened leaves are too hard for most animals to chew.

- Spines, thorns, and prickles keep animals at a distance.

- Nasty tasting or poisonous chemicals make sure the animal does not eat the same plant again.

There are two main groups of trees. Conifers, or cone-bearing trees, are known as softwoods and keep their leaves throughout the year. Broad-leaved trees are hardwoods, and those growing in cool climates lose their leaves in autumn. Trees play a vital role in maintaining life on Earth, because their leaves give off oxygen as part of the tree's food-making process.

How can you tell a bush from a shrub?

Shrubs are small, tree-like plants while bushes have more branches than shrubs, and are usually smaller. Shrubs have woody stems and several branches, spreading out near to the ground. Gardeners often grow bush roses, fruit bushes such as blueberries, and ornamental shrubs such as fuchsias, azaleas, and rhododendrons. Shrubs provide useful cover for wildlife, especially birds and small mammals.

🔽 *Woodland with a mixture of trees and shrubs is a good habitat for animals.*

Why do some trees lose their leaves?

🔼 *Autumn leaves provide a brilliant colour show as the trees prepare for winter.*

Losing their leaves in autumn helps trees save water as they "shut down" their food-gathering system in winter. Food pipes inside the tree branches are sealed. Enough food has been stored within the tree to make buds grow in the spring. The leaf is cut off from its food supply and dies. The chlorophyll that keeps it green breaks down, and the leaves turn red, yellow, and brown, before they fall to the ground.

Tree **facts**

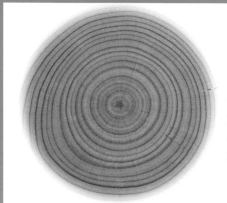

🔼 *Annual growth rings can be seen when a tree is cut. The tree adds a new ring every year.*

Leaves absorb sunlight, which helps to create food for the plant

➡ *The different parts of a tree all work together to provide water, sunlight, protection, and fruit.*

Apple tree

Blossoms are pollinated to develop into fruit

Minerals and water in the soil are absorbed by the roots

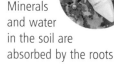

Tubes in the bark carry water and sap, which is rich in energy, to all parts of the plant

Why do trees have bark?

Bark protects the living wood inside the tree. It keeps moisture in, so the tree does not dry out. It protects the tree from insects and parasites, and shields against extreme weather. The outer layer of bark is a tough, dead shell. The inner layer is soft and alive, and carries food through tiny tubes.

Where are the biggest forests?

The biggest forests are the tropical rainforest of Brazil and the cold boreal forest of Siberia. Many trees growing together make a forest. Once 60 percent of the Earth was forested, but humans have cleared much of the ancient forest to build on. Forests are home to many plants and animals.

⬇ *Forest life exists in layers from the floor through the shrub and understory to the canopy (the tallest trees).*

Why do conifer trees bear cones?

Male cones produce pollen, female cones produce eggs, which are sticky and attract the pollen. All conifer trees have cones. Seeds are made in the scales of the female cone, and spread by the wind. Most conifers are evergreen and grow best in cool climates. Typical conifers include spruce, pine, and firs.

⬆ *Redwood trees have soft, spongy bark and are one of the tallest trees.*

⬇ *Conifers can grow in places where there is little water (or where the water is frozen in winter). Having thin leaves means they lose little moisture.*

Coast redwood

Silver fir

Italian cypress

Cedar of Lebanon

Norway spruce

Stone pine

Amazing **tree facts**

• The heaviest tree is the giant sequoia "General Sherman," growing in California. Its weight is estimated at 2,750 tons.

• A Douglas fir cut down in British Columbia, Canada, in the 19th century was 420 ft. high.

• The oldest living trees are bristlecone pines found in the mountains of California. They are believed to live for 5,000 years.

• The oldest species of tree is the gingko or maidenhair. Fossil leaves of this tree dating from 160 million years ago have been found.

• Probably the weirdest-looking tree is the baobab. Its bottle-shaped trunk, used for storing water, can measure 165 ft. in diameter.

• The banyan tree of India grows aerial roots that hang down from the branches to the ground, forming a miniforest up to 2,000 ft. wide.

➡ *The strange looking baobab tree.*

People need plants, as sources of food, for raw materials, for fuel, and to maintain the natural balance of the planet. Many plants have been altered by people through selective breeding. This process began when people first became farmers, about 10,000 years ago. Today's farm crops look very different from their wild ancestors.

⬆ *The sunflower turns its head throughout the day, following the Sun's path across the sky.*

Why are sunflowers useful as well as pretty?

Sunflowers produce useful foodstuffs, such as sunflower oil and sunflower seeds. Sunflowers have inspired artists, and children like to grow them to see how tall they become. A field full of sunflowers makes a brilliant sight, a mass of yellow blooms. So sunflowers are both a useful crop and a popular flower to grow.

What are tubers?

Tubers are food stores, and probably the best-known tuberous plant is the potato. The tuber is the thick, swollen part of the stem, which grows underground. Potatoes were unknown in Europe until the first explorers brought them back from America in the 1500s. The eyes of a potato are tiny buds, which will sprout and grow into new plants if put into the soil.

➡ *Gardeners "earth up" the plants to make sure the tubers are covered by soil for plants such as this potato plant.*

⬆ *Vast areas of what was once prairie in North America is now planted with wheat, one of the most important world crops.*

Which plants are staple foods?

Staple foods make up the largest part of a person's diet and include potatoes, wheat (made into bread and pasta), and rice. Potatoes and wheat are popular in western countries, while people in poorer parts of Africa and Asia rely almost entirely on plants such as rice, cassava, and yams.

Fruit, vegetables, and **firewood**

Working the land
In poorer countries, about half the population works on the land. Many are subsistence farmers—this means they grow just enough food to feed themselves and their families.

In richer countries, the number of people employed on farms is much less—under 10 percent of the population on average. In the developing world, many people burn wood for fuel. About 90 percent of the timber cut in India is burned for cooking on wood-stoves. Timber is used for construction, furniture, and (as pulp) for making paper for newsprint. In well-managed forests new young trees are planted to replace the mature trees cut down. But many tropical forests are being felled thoughtlessly for quick profits.

⬆ *Harvesting by machine means a farmer needs few workers.*

→ *Terraced rice fields are a common sight in many parts of Asia.*

Which parts of plants can we eat?

The roots, bulbs, flowering heads, and leaves of some plants are edible. Cauliflower and broccoli are the flowering heads of plants belonging to the cabbage family. Onions are bulbs. Carrots and parsnips are roots. We eat the leaves of lettuces, and the fruits of many plants, such as apples. Some plants are dangerous to eat—rhubarb leaves, for example, are poisonous, though the stems can be eaten. Mistletoe berries are poisonous, and so are yew and laburnum seeds.

⬇ *Pineapples are grown in Central America, Asia, Australia, and Africa. The bit we eat is the fruit, which is normally seedless.*

⬇ *Rice is a cereal, like wheat, which needs warm, wet conditions in which to grow.*

How is rice cultivated?

Young rice plants are grown in flooded "paddy" fields and the water is drained off before the rice is harvested. More than half the world's population eat rice as their main food. Once harvested, the rice grains are boiled and eaten, rather than ground into flour (like wheat grains).

Can we eat seaweed?

Seaweed is rich in vitamins and minerals, and many kinds are good to eat. In Wales, a red seaweed known as laver is boiled up into a jellylike mass, fried, and eaten as "laver bread." The Japanese pioneered seaweed farming. Seaweed farmers drive rows of stakes into the shallow seabed to provide the plant with something to cling to. When the seaweed is harvested, it is used as an ingredient in various foods. If you see the names agar, algin, or carrageenin on food packages, you will know those products contain seaweed.

→ *A farmer harvesting seaweed, which is used in many food and cosmetic products. Ice cream is one of many foods that may contain seaweed.*

First-grown **vegetables**

Vegetable	Date first grown
Pea	9000 BC
Wheat	7000 BC
Rye	6500 BC
Runner bean	5000 BC
Barley	4500 BC
Lettuce	4500 BC
Radish	3000 BC
Rice	3000 BC

Radishes

Lettuce

World food **production**

Top rice producers: China, India, Indonesia
Top potato growers: Russia, Poland, China
Top sugar producers: Brazil, India, Russia
Top wine producers: Italy, France, Spain

Continent	Produces and exports
Asia	43 percent
Europe (including Russia)	27 percent
U.S.A. and Canada	11 percent
Africa	7 percent
Oceania (including Australia)	2 percent

In order to find food, escape danger, and to reproduce successfully, animals use a variety of natural strategies. For example, camouflage and protective coloration enable some animals to escape being seen or to appear so visibly that a predator is startled or scared away. The range of animal defenses is amazing, from armadillo armor, porcupine's quills, mimicry, and camouflage to lobster claws and the skunk's foul-smelling spray.

⬆ *Baby loggerhead turtles head for deep water. Many turtles are killed by waiting predators.*

Where do marine turtles lay their eggs?

Marine turtles lay their eggs on sandy beaches. The females dig a shallow hole, lay the eggs, cover them with sand, then crawl back to the water. When the babies hatch, they have to dig their way up to the light and air. They head straight for the water because waiting on the shore are a host of predators, such as seabirds, that seem to know just when the hatchlings will emerge.

⬇ *Woodland animals hibernate during the winter months, only emerging when the weather warms up. Badgers go into a deep sleep but don't truly hibernate. They sometimes stay in their underground setts for long periods of time.*

Why do some animals hibernate?

Hibernation is a strategy for surviving winter, when food is scarce. Hibernating animals live off the reserves of fat stored in their bodies until warmer weather awakens them. Bears that live in cold climates fatten themselves up in autumn, then sleep in a cozy den. Some animals, such as dormice, shut down their bodies so much that they appear to be dead.

Survival **champions**

⬇ *Some nonvenomous snakes, such as this green snake, mimic poisonous snakes as a method of defence. Predators are warned off, thinking it to be dangerous.*

Safest when seen
Not all animals choose to hide from danger. Some make sure they can be seen.

Bees and wasps are boldly marked with black and yellow stripes to warn birds that if they peck they risk being stung.

Poisonous animals, such as the poison arrow frog and coral snakes, are often vividly colored, too, to warn off predators.

Some animals with no real defenses "mimic" animals that are dangerous. There are flies that are harmless, but that look just like wasps and there are harmless milk snakes that look like poisonous coral snakes.

The bee orchid flower looks like a bee—to attract male bees eager to mate, making sure its pollen gets carried away.

Why do some mammals live in groups?

Living together in a group is a good defensive strategy. An antelope has a better chance of escaping a lion if it stays in a herd—lots of eyes keeping watch are better than just one pair. Elephants have no real enemies (except some humans), but female elephants stay together to share the task of bringing up the young. Lions, unlike most cats, cooperate when hunting. So do wolves, wild dogs, and hyenas who hunt in "packs."

⊙ *A herd of elephants is usually led by an old female—the matriarch cow. The herd will look after an injured member and protect the young from predators such as lions.*

Why do animals build homes?

Many animals have territories, but homes are usually only for rearing young. Females prepare a den or a nest for their young. Birds make the most ingenious homes, mostly in treetops or bushes. Fish, such as the male stickleback, guard their young fiercely. One of the most remarkable mammal homes is the beaver's underwater lodge. Built from mud and sticks, the lodge provides a dry, weatherproof home safe from land predators.

⊙ *North American beavers dam streams by cutting down small trees to make a pond. In the pond, they make their lodge with an underwater entrance.*

What is migration?

Animals such as whales, fish, lobsters, caribou, and butterflies all migrate— make seasonal journeys—to find reliable food supplies and the best breeding places.

The most remarkable migrants are birds, and many species migrate as the seasons change. Songbirds, seabirds, waterfowl, and waders all migrate.

⊙ *The Arctic tern is the most-traveled bird. It breeds in the Arctic during the northern summer, then flies south for summer in the Antarctic. The round trip covers more than 15,500 miles.*

⊙ *Marine iguanas are the only reptiles to feed in the ocean. They dive into the sea to browse on seaweed, then crawl back onto the rocks to warm up in the sunshine.*

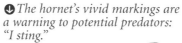

⊙ *The hornet's vivid markings are a warning to potential predators: "I sting."*

Animal **hibernation**

Bats—find a dry cave to sleep in because in winter, there are few insects to feed on.

Stoats—normally brown, turn white in winter – this camouflages them in the snow.

Frogs, toads, newts, and snakes—hibernate in crevices in rocks or trees.

Squirrels—collect a store of nuts in autumn to last the winter. They do not hibernate completely, waking up on mild days.

Hedgehogs—curl up inside piles of dead leaves, waking on milder days.

The record breakers in the natural world come in all shapes and sizes. Many animals are unbelievably strong. Some insects and mammals have incredible appetites. The fastest animals can easily outrun a human sprinter. And no creature in the history of the Earth has been bigger than the majestic blue whale.

The peregrine falcon reaches maximum speed in a dive to catch prey.

What is the world's fastest animal?

The peregrine falcon, which in a dive or "stoop" on its prey can reach a speed of more than 125 mph. Ducks are probably the fastest fliers in level flight, reaching up to 60 mph. The cheetah is the fastest land animal and the sailfish is the fastest fish, both clocking in at approximately 60 to 70 mph. The cheetah cannot keep up its sprint for long, whereas the pronghorn antelope can sustain a speed of over 40 mph for longer. In comparison, a top Olympic sprinter can reach about 25 mph.

What is the world's biggest big cat?

The Siberian tiger is the biggest of the big cats. It is the most northern species of tiger, at home in the snow. It can measure 10 ft. from nose to tail and weigh up to 660 lb. Carnivores (meat eaters) include some of the most powerful predators in the animal world. The biggest land carnivores are bears and big cats.

What is the largest cactus?

Most cacti are fairly small, but the saguaro is an exception at a height of 60 ft. It grows in the deserts of Arizona, California, and Mexico. The saguaro has a column-like trunk from which sprout upturned branches. A big one can weigh up to 10 tons.

The saguaro cactus is as tall as a tree.

The Siberian tiger is a magnificent animal. It is an endangered species (at risk of extinction) and needs protection from hunters.

Remarkable record-breakers

Bristlecone pines are the world's oldest trees, up to 5,000 years old.

The giraffe has very long legs, but its neck earns it a place in the record book.

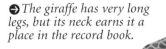

The most fearsome jaws are those of the great white shark.

Fastest movers

Peregrine falcon	125 mph
Canvasback duck	68 mph
Sailfish	68 mph
Cheetah	62 mph
Swift	59 mph
Gazelle	50 mph
Lion	50 mph
Jackrabbit	43 mph
Pronghorn antelope	43 mph
Racehorse	43 mph

Which are the most deadly sea animals?

Perhaps the most deadly sea creature to humans is the sea wasp jellyfish with a sting that can kill a person in less than 3 minutes. The most feared hunters of the ocean are great white sharks and killer whales, which eat seals and sea lions, and will even attack larger whales. Sharks lurk off seal beaches during the breeding season, while killer whales pursue fleeing seals into shallow surf and grab them off the beach itself. However, more people are killed every year by jellyfish than either of these larger animals.

➔ *The sea wasp jellyfish.*

What are the smallest animals?

The smallest bird is the 2 in.-long bee hummingbird, the smallest reptile is the dwarf gecko at half that size, and the smallest amphibian, the short-headed frog is just 0.3 in. long. The smallest horse, the Falabella, is only the size of a dog. Small means safe sometimes, for a small animal can hide where no large predator can follow. However, there are weasels small enough to pursue mice down their holes. There are tiny flies that lay their eggs on the bodies of larger flies. There are a whole host of minibeasts, some of which can be seen only under a microscope.

⬆ *Killer whales grab seals from shallow water and from along the shore's edge.*

⬆ *The world's smallest gecko at 1 in., and the world's smallest frog at just 0.4 in., shown to scale on a human hand.*

Most massive **predators**

Name	Length	Weight
Killer whale	30 ft.	19,800 lb.
Great white shark	15 ft.	7,275 lb.
Elephant seal	16 ft.	5,075 lb.

Animal **records**

Longest worm	North sea bootlace worm	180 ft. long
Biggest spider	Bird-eating spider	11 in. across
Biggest mollusc	Giant squid	56 ft. long
Biggest crab	Japanese spider crab	6.5 ft. across

Amazing **animal facts**

- The biggest land animal is the African elephant. A big bull (male) weighs more than 7 tons.

- The blue whale (heaviest recorded weight 209 tons), gives birth to the biggest baby. At birth, a whale calf is already 20–26 ft. long.

- The giraffe is the tallest mammal, with the longest neck—a giraffe can reach 20 ft. above the ground to reach juicy leaves.

- The Goliath beetle is the heaviest insect at 150–220 lb.

- The animals with most legs are centipedes and millipedes. Millipedes have the most, up to 370 pairs. But centipedes run faster.

Why not test your knowledge of the natural world! Try answering these questions to find out how much you know about reptiles, mammals, birds and camouflage, plant records, trees, flowering plants, and much more. Questions are grouped into the subject areas covered within the pages of this book. See how much you remember, and discover how much more you can learn by looking at other sources to help you answer these questions.

17 A giant tortoise, which can grow up to 4 ft. long, comes from which group of islands in the Pacific Ocean?

The Animal Kingdom

1 Is an animal that eats meat called a herbivore, a carnivore, or an omnivore?
2 Do reptiles create their own body heat, or do they absorb it from the Sun and surroundings?
3 Which gas, essential to animal life, is produced by green plants: hydrogen, oxygen, or carbon dioxide?

Prehistoric Animals

4 Did *Tyrannosaurus rex* sometimes walk on four legs?
5 Which came first: dinosaurs or birds?
6 Which animal were prehistoric woolly mammoths similar to: rhinos, elephants, or sheep?

Mammals

8 Which is larger, the African or the Asian elephant?
9 Do seals give birth at sea or on land?
10 Which furry animal flies on wings of skin?

Birds

11 Which is larger: a duck or a goose?
12 Can seagulls swim under water?
13 What does a cygnet grow into?

Reptiles and Amphibians

14 What baby reptile squeaks inside its egg: a lizard, crocodile, or snake?
15 Do frogs hunt mainly by smell, hearing, or sight?
16 Which turtles regularly return to the same spot to lay their eggs?

Fish

18 Are swordfish river or sea fish?
19 Does the parrot fish talk, or have beak-like teeth?
20 Do pike swim in shoals or live alone?

Invertebrate Animals

21 Do earthworms eat insects or dead plant material?
22 What is a tarantula?
23 Which sea creature usually has five limbs?

7 Which dinosaur, beginning with "s," could grow up to 160 ft. long and weigh up to 90 tons?

24 Do most fungi like to grow in bright, dry areas, or in dark, damp areas?

Using Plants

37 Which vegetable does not grow underground: carrot, pea, or potato?

38 Which vegetable is made into a Hallowe'en lantern?

39 Which member of the grass family provides Asia's main food crop: wheat, rye, or rice?

Natural Strategies

40 How do poison-dart frogs warn off enemies: with bright colors, by hissing or by swelling up?

41 How do penguins recognize their young: by their appearance, their voice, or their smell?

42 When do rattlesnakes rattle: when they are tired, to threaten enemies, or when they are ready to breed?

Endangered Animals

25 Was the dodo a type of bird or deer?

26 Which of the big cats has seen its numbers drop from 50,000 in the early 1900s to fewer than 6,000 left today?

27 Which bear has been reduced in number because of deforestation?

Flowering Plants

31 Do bluebells grow on beaches or in woods?

32 Which are taller, foxgloves or bluebells?

33 Which large yellow flower is used in the making of cooking oil: marigold, sunflower, or daffodil?

Animal and Plant Records

43 What is the world's largest bird?

44 Which is the world's largest frog: the African bullfrog, the Goliath frog, or the giant tree frog?

45 What is the world's biggest eagle: the golden eagle, the harpy eagle, or the bald eagle?

Plants and Fungi

28 The sundew plant catches prey on its sticky tentacles: true or false?

29 A pitcher plant catches and eats insects: true or false?

30 Which of these is a type of plant: sponge, coral, or kelp?

Trees and Shrubs

34 Are acorns the seeds of the oak or the holly?

35 Do coconuts grow on plants or on trees?

36 Do willow trees like damp or dry conditions?

Answers

1 Carnivore
2 They absorb heat
3 Carbon dioxide
4 No, its front legs were too tiny
5 Dinosaurs
6 Elephants
7 *Seismosaurus*
8 African elephant
9 On land
10 Bat
11 Goose
12 No

13 Swan
14 Crocodile
15 Sight
16 Sea turtles
17 The Galapagos Islands
18 Sea fish
19 Beak-like teeth
20 Live alone
21 Dead plant material
22 Spider (or arachnid)
23 Starfish
24 Dark, damp areas

25 Bird
26 Tiger
27 Giant panda
28 True
29 True
30 Kelp, which is a kind of seaweed
31 In woods
32 Foxgloves
33 Sunflower
34 Oak
35 On trees
36 Damp conditions

37 Pea
38 Pumpkin
39 Rice
40 With bright colors
41 Their voice
42 To threaten enemies
43 Ostrich
44 Goliath frog—up to 16 in. in length
45 Harpy eagle

Page numbers in **bold** refer to main subjects, page numbers in *italics* refer to illustrations.

A

Africa 14, 30
African elephant 9, *9*, 11, 35
albatrosses 14, *14*
algae 8, 9, 25
alligators 16
amoebas 8, *8*
amphibians 9, **16–17**, *16–17*
  eggs 16
  smallest 35, *35*
angiosperms 24, 25
anglerfish 19, *19*
animals **8–9**, *8–9*
  biggest 35
  endangered species **22–23**, *22–23*, 34
  fastest 34
  most intelligent 12, 15
  record breakers 13, **34–35**
  smallest 35
Antarctica 15
arachnids *see* spiders
Arctic tern 33, *33*
Asia 30, 31
Asian elephant 9
Australia 12, 14
axolotl 17, *17*

B

baboons 12
bacteria 8, 9
badgers 12
bamboo 25, *25*
bandicoots 12
bats 13, *13*, 27, 33
beaks 15
beans 24
bears 23
  polar bears 13, 15
beavers 33, *33*
bees 21, *21*, 27, *27*
birds 9, **14–15**, *14–15*, 27, 33
  biggest 14
  fastest 34
  oldest 15
  smallest 35
birth 13, 35
blue whale 12, 34, 35
bolas spider 20, *20*
bombardier beetle 20, *20*
Brazil 29

bristlecone pine 29, 34, *34*
bryophytes 25
bushes 28

C

cacti 26, *26*, 34, *34*
  biggest 34, *34*
  saguaro 34, *34*
canopy *see* trees
carnivores 9, 12, 34
carnivorous plants 25
cartilage 18
cassowaries 14
caterpillars *20*, 21
cats 13, 34
cattail fungus 25, *25*
cells 8, 9, 24, 26
chameleons 17, *17*
cheetahs 12, 34
chimpanzees 12
chlorophyll 24, 25, 28
chrysalises 20, *20*
clams 20
cocoons 21, *21*
coelacanths 19, *19*
cold-blooded animals 16
compositae 24
cones 29
conifers 24, 28, 29, *29*
cookie-cutter shark 19, *19*
corals 20
crab, hermit 20, *20*
crocodiles 16–17, *16–17*
  gharial 16
cross-pollination 27
crustaceans 9, 20
cycads 24, *24*

D

dandelions 27, *27*
deepsea fish 18–19, *18–19*
defenses
  of animals 32–33
  of dinosaurs 10
  of plants 27
desert plants 26
diatoms 8, *8*
dinosaurs 10–11, *10–11*, 22
  Allosaurus 10
  Ankylosaurus 11
  Archaeopteryx 10, *10*
  Baluchitherium 11
  biggest 10, 11
  Brachiosaurus 10, 11, *11*

dinosaurs *(continued)*
  ceratopsian 10, *10*
  Diplodocus 10
  eggs 10, *10*
  Maiasaura 10, *10*
  Mamenchisaurus 11
  pterosaur 11
  ornithischian hip bones 11, *11*
  saurischian hip bones 11, *11*
  Seismosaurus 10, 11
  Tyrannosaurus rex 11, *11*
DNA (deoxyribonucleic acid) 8, *8*
dodos 23, *23*
dogfish 18, *18*
dogs 12, 23
dolphins 12–13, *12–13*
dragonfish 19, *19*
dragonflies 11, 20, *20*
duck-billed platypus 12, *12*

E

echidnas 12
eggs 14, 15
  amphibians 16
  birds 15
  dinosaurs 10, *10*
  fish 18
  mammals 12
  reptiles 16, *16*
  turtles 32
elephants 9, *9*, 10, 13, 33, *33*
  African 9, *9*, 11, 35
  Asian 9
emus 14
endangered animals **22–23**, *22–23*, 34
evolutionary change 8–9, *8–9*
extinctions 10, 22, 23

F

farming 30–31, *30–31*
feathers 10, 11, 14
feeding 9
ferns 24, *24*
fish 9, 12, 13, 15, **18–19**, *18–19*
  anglerfish 19, *19*
  biggest 18
  deepsea fish 18–19, *18–19*
  devilfish 19, *19*
  dogfish 18, *18*
  dragonfish 19, *19*
  eggs 18
  giant oarfish 19, *19*
  heaviest 18
  lantern fish 19, *19*

fish (continued)
longest 19
piranha 18, *18*
scales 19
sunfish 18, *18*
tails 19, *19*
viperfish 18–19, *18–19*
yellow snappers 18, *18*
flight **14–15**, *14–15*
flower parts 26, *26*
flowering plants 9, 24, 25, **26–27**, *26–27*
biggest 26
flying reptiles 10, *10*, 11
food 30–31, *30–31*
forests 22, 29, 30
biggest 29
fossils 8, 10, *10*
foxes 9, 12
frilled lizard 16, *16*
frogs 13, 16, *16*, 17, *17*, 33
fruit 28
fungi 8, **24–25**, *24–25*, 26
cattail fungus 25, *25*
deadliest 25

G

gharial 16
geckos 17, 35
germination 26, *26*
gestation periods 13
longest 13
giant oarfish 19, *19*
giant panda 22, *22*
gingkos 24, 29
giraffes 12, 13, 34, *34*, 35
gorillas 8, *8*, 12
grass, tallest 25
great white shark 34, *34*, 35
green mantis 21, *21*
gymnosperms 24, 25

H

habitat 28
destruction of 22
hardwoods 28
harvesting crops 30, *30*, 31
herbivores 9
hermit crab 20, *20*
hibernation 16, 32, *32*, 33
hippopotamuses 12, 13
homes, animal 33
hoofed animals, biggest 12, 13
horns, cutting off 23

horses 8–9, *8–9*, 35
humans 8, 22, 29, 35
hummingbirds 14, 15, 35
eggs 15

I

iguanas, marine 33, *33*
insects 9, 13, 20–21, *20–21*, 27, 29, 34, 35
biggest 21
fastest running 21
heaviest 21, 35
longest 21
with most legs 35
invertebrate animals **20–21**, *20–21*

J

jackals 12
jaguars 12
Jurassic Period 8, *8*

K

kangaroos 12, *12*
killer whale 13, *13*, 15, 35, *35*
kiwis 14
koalas 22, *22*
Komodo dragon 16, *16*

L

lantern fish 19, *19*
leaves 27, *27*
trees 28, *28*
legumes 24
leopard seal 15
leopards 12–13, *12–13*
snow leopard 22, *22*
lions 12, 23
lizards 17, *17*
frilled lizard 16, *16*
tails 16, *16*
loggerhead turtles 32, *32*

M

mammals 8, 9, **12–13**, *12–13*, 15, 34
biggest group 13
biggest mammal 12
eggs 12
groups 33
sea-dwelling 13
mandrills 9, *9*
manta rays 19, *19*

mantis, green 21, *21*
maple trees 27
marsupials 12, 27
metamorphosis 20
migration 33
mink 12
moas 14, 23, *23*
molluscs 9, 20, 35
monera 8
monocotyledons 26
mosses 24, 27
moths 20, 21, *21*
mushrooms 26

N

natural strategies **32–33**
New Guinea 12, 14
New Zealand 14
newts 17, 33
nonflowering plants 9, 24
North America 12, 23, 33

O

oceans 8, 10
oil spills 23
omnivores 9
opossums 12
orangutans 12, 13
orchids 24, 25, 32
ostriches 14, *14*, 15
otters 12
oxygen 24, 28

P

panda, giant 22, *22*
peas 24
penguins 15, *15*
peregrine falcon 34, *34*
photosynthesis 8, 24, *24*, 26
pigeons 23
pineapples 31, *31*
pinnipeds 9
piranha 18, *18*
pitcher plants 25, *25*
plants 9, **24–25**, *24–25*
biggest 25
edible 31
families 25
flowering plants **26–27**, *26–27*
growth 26–27, *26–27*
mountain plants 27
oldest 25
record breakers 34

plants (continued)
  using plants **30–31**, *30–31*
  water-dwelling 25
platypus, duck-billed 12, *12*
poaching 23
polar bear 13, 15
pollen 27
possums 12
potatoes 30, *30*
pouched animals 12, *12*
prehistoric animals **10–11**, *10–11*
protists 8
pteridophytes 25
pythons 17

R
rafflesia 26, *26*
record breakers 13, 21, **34–35**
reproduction 8
reptiles 9, 10, 11, 15, **16–17**, *16–17*
  biggest 16
  eggs 16, *16*
  smallest 35, *35*
rheas 14
rhinoceroses 13, *13*, 23, *23*
  white rhinoceros 12
rice 30, 31, *31*
rodents 13
roots 27
roundworms 9

S
saguaro cactus 34, *34*
salamanders 17
sea animals
  deadliest 35
sea lions 9, 13
sea wasp jellyfish 35, *35*
seabirds 23, 33
seals 9, 13, 35, *35*
  leopard seal 15
seaweed 25, *25*, 31, *31*
seeds 24, 29
  winged 27

sharks 12, 18
  cookie-cutter shark 19, *19*
  great white shark 34, *34*, 35
  whale shark 18, *18*
shells, biggest 20
shoals 18
shrubs 27, **28–29**, *28–29*
Siberian tiger 34, *34*
singing, birds 15
snakes 16, *16*, 17, *17*, 32, *32*, 33
  longest 17
snow leopard 22, *22*
social groups 33
softwoods 28
songthrush 15, *15*
South America 12, 14
species 9
  endangered **22–23**, *22–23*, 34
  fish 18
  insects 20, 21
  plants 24, 25
  reptiles 16
spiders 9, 20, 35
  bolas spider 20, *20*
spiny anteater 12
spores 24, *24*, 25
staple foods 30
starfish 20
storks 14, 15, *15*
sunfish 18, *18*
sunflowers 30, *30*
survival **32–33**, *32–33*

T
teeth 15
territories 15, 33
tigers 12, 23
  Siberian tiger 34, *34*
timber 30
toads 17, 33
tortoises 17, *17*
transpiration 27
trees 8, 28–29, *28–29*
  annual growth rings 28, *28*
  apple 28, *28*

trees (continued)
  baobab trees 29, *29*
  bark 28, *28*, 29
  canopy 29
  heaviest 29
  maple 27
  oldest 29
  redwood 29, *29*
  tallest 29
  understory 29
tubers 30
tulips 27, *27*
turtles 22, *22*, 23
  eggs 32
  loggerhead turtles 32, *32*

V
vegetables 31
vertebrate animals 14, 20
viperfish 18–19

W
wallabies 12
walruses 9, *9*, 13
warm-blooded animals 14
wasps 32, *33*
water 24, 25, 26
water lilies 25, *25*
weasels 35
whale shark 18, *18*
whales 8, 12, 13, 22
  blue whale 12, 34, 35
  killer whale 13, *13*, 15, 35, *35*
wheat 30, *30*
white rhinoceros 12
wind 27
wisteria 26
wolves 12, 23
wombats 12
woodland 28, *28*
worms 9, 35

The publishers would like to thank the following artists who have contributed to this book:
Lisa Alderson, Syd Brak, Chris Buzer, Martin Camm, Mark Davis, Peter Dennis, Fiammetta Dogi/Galante Studio, Richard Draper, Wayne Ford, Chris Forsey, Luigi Galante Studio, Alan Hancocks, Alan Harris, Ron Hayward, Ian Jackson, Stuart Lafford, Mick Loates, Kevin Maddison, Alan Male, Doreen McGuiness, A.Menchi/Galante Studio, Andrea Morandi, Terry Riley, Steve Roberts, Eric Robson, Mike Saunders, Sarah Smith, Rudi Vizi, Mike White, Colin Wolf

All photographs are from:
Corbis, Corel, digitalvision, John Foxx, Photoalto